Memoirs of a

BOOBLESS WOMAN

Memoirs of a
BOOBLESS
WOMAN

by Martha Sherman

MEMOIRS OF A BOOBLESS WOMAN

Martha Sherman
marthaksherman@gmail.com

ACKNOWLEDGEMENTS

Unless otherwise indicated, Scripture quotations are from the HOLY BIBLE, NEW INTERNATIONAL VERSION. Copyright ©1973, 1978, 1984 by International Bible Society. Used by permission of Zondervan Publishing House. All rights reserved.

Scripture quotations identified as The Message are from THE MESSAGE VERSION. Copyright © by Eugene H. Peterson, 1993, 1994, 1995. Used by permission of NavPress Publishing Group.

1st edition
ISBN: 978-1-304-52145-3

Cover design by Mike Sherman, Isaiah Sherman, and Cherish Sherman

To my husband, Mike Sherman. You have walked with me for the last 35 years, never leaving my side even when times were difficult and the future unknown. Thank you for showing me what Jesus looks like in a man.

And in honor of my mother, Helen Nye, who died of cancer in 1990. The climbing clematis flower on the cover of this book is in loving memory of you.

CONTENTS

Forward	1
The Journey Begins	4
September 2006	7
October 2006	10
December 2006	12
January 2007	19
February 2007	31
March 2007	40
April 2006	46
May 2007	57
June 2007	67
July 2007	72
August 2007	81
September 2007	83
October 2007	84
December 2007	87
January 2008	88
February 2008	89
March 2008	90
Afterword	93
About the Author	95

FORWARD

It is not safe for me to write this book. I mean, the title alone is risqué. Sharing and writing about one's boobs is definitely not your ordinary read. It's risky putting my personal thoughts and feelings out there for the world to read, but if we never take risks we will never know the joy or the exhilaration of the experience afterwards.

This is coming from one of the safest people alive. I'm what you call a toe-tester type. You know, never jumping in before testing the waters. I don't like it too hot or too cold. I need a plan. Spontaneity stresses me out! But let me plan, make lists and mediate on something for awhile, and I'm in my element.

The Lord has been working on me for a long time now, and has helped me in this area. Oh, I'm still far away from being the adventurous type, but I have learned to take some risks along the way. He has helped me learn to face my fears over the years, not always at my own choosing.

Looking back, I can see now that I never really lived as a young woman. I was too afraid to try anything new, too afraid of failing, too afraid of getting hurt. Life has dealt me some hands where I was forced to face some ugly things. Yes, I was hurt both physically and emotionally, yet I lived through it all. And, in the process, I grew and changed and matured.

In taking risks, I learned that there is some fun to be had out there. I think the biggest reward was learning to take a risk to help someone else, to reach out and offer some encouragement.

I remember the first time I actually told someone that I would be praying for them. That was huge for me. The words didn't want to come out of my mouth, but I took a risk and said them. The woman I was talking with was so appreciative and I could see in her eyes a hope that wasn't there a moment before.

That was only the beginning. The Lord has seen fit to use me in many areas involving helping and encouraging others. Oh there have been many times I've been too afraid to do something that I knew He wanted me to do and I was disappointed in myself and never saw the blessing that it could have been to someone else. But, when I am obedient, follow my heart, and take that risk, I am always blessed by blessing someone else.

I've felt for a long time now that I was to share my journal to encourage others going through breast cancer. I wish I had a book that would have encouraged me when I started on my journey through cancer. I felt alone because I knew no one who had done what I did. It was a risky move to have both of my breasts removed at the same time.

So, although it is risky on my part, I write this book in the hope of encouraging others. If my experience encourages only one, then my risk has been worth it.

Isaiah 55: 8-12: "'For my thoughts are not your thoughts, neither are your ways my ways,' declares the Lord. 'As the heavens are higher than the earth, so are my ways higher than your ways and my thoughts than your thoughts. As the rain and the snow come down from heaven, and do not return to it without watering the earth and making it bud and flourish, so that it yields seed for the sower and bread for the eater, so is my word that goes out from my mouth: It will not return to me empty, but will accomplish what I desire

2

and achieve the purpose for which I sent it. You will go out in joy and be led forth in peace.' "

As you read this book, my prayer is that you would be encouraged and lifted up through God's word and His promises. God's word is alive! May His word be planted deep in your soul and begin to grow and develop new life and a new hope within you.

All my love,
Martha

THE JOURNEY BEGINS

Seven years ago I began on a journey that I would like to share with you. My hope is that my personal walk through breast cancer will encourage those who are embarking on that same journey. I really can't begin this story without some personal history.

So, let's see where should I begin? I guess I would have to say that it all began when I was pregnant with my fourth baby. I was twenty-seven years old and only a couple of months pregnant. We were camping as a family at a local campsite, when I began to bleed out of one of my nipples. I was very surprised and frightened at the same time. You can imagine all the thoughts that started going through my head.

After informing my doctor, I was scheduled for a mammogram, my first of many to come. I'll never forget that appointment.

The woman who was doing the mammogram placed an iron apron over my belly "to protect the baby from the radiation," she said. Then she grumbled under her breath, loudly enough for me to hear though, "As if it will do any good." She obviously did not agree to a pregnant woman getting a mammogram.

So, needless to say, I was very anxious not only about the bleeding, but now I was concerned for my unborn child as well.

The diagnoses turned out to be "Intraductal Papillomatosis." This is a condition where small, wart size, non-cancerous growths grow inside the milk ducts. I was told by my doctor I had twice the risk of a normal woman to get breast cancer in my lifetime.

When my baby was turning 1 year old, a lump appeared in my right breast. It was the first of many lumps, all of which I had removed. Between the ages of twenty-eight and thirty-eight, I had five breast biopsies. All were benign growths. I had to have a mammogram every six months through those years.

My doctor actually told me we had to cut back on the mammograms as I was getting too much radiation exposure. (I read later after being diagnosed with breast cancer that too many mammograms can actually put a woman at a greater risk of getting breast cancer) Too late now.

I had always been a well-endowed young woman. I did not really enjoy that feature of my body, but it was how God made me. No one else in my family was built like me, nor had I ever heard of any other woman in our family getting breast cancer.

My mother died of cancer, but it was diagnosed in the very late stages, and it had turned into bone cancer by then. She was also a smoker. We will never know what kind of cancer she had as it was all over her body when she was finally diagnosed with it. That is a totally different story.

At the age of thirty-nine, I finally got the breast reduction I had always wanted. My family physician had recommended I have it done several times through the years, but it was a very big decision to make. Finally I was ready and my husband was very supportive of me. I had no further lumps appear after the breast reduction until eight years later, December 2006.

I have written several journals through the years. I love reading back through them to see who I was and what I was thinking at the time. It's a good way to see how one has grown. I have not been consistent in my journals though. They are a sporadic collection.

In September of 2006, I began reading the *NIV One Year Bible* devotional. Certain scriptures of God's promises began to jump out at me, so I started another journal and wrote them down as they spoke to me.

Journal Entries
SEPTEMBER 2006

Sept. 26

<u>Isaiah 39:10</u>: "So do not fear, for I am with you; do not be dismayed for I am your God. I will strengthen you and help you; I will uphold you with my righteous right hand".

<u>Ephesians 1:11</u>: "…having been predestined according to the plan of Him who works out EVERYTHING in conformity with the purpose of His will".

Sept. 30

<u>Isaiah 60:1-3:</u> "Arise, shine, for your light has come and the glory of the Lord rises upon you. See darkness covers the earth and thick darkness is over the peoples, but The Lord rises upon you and His glory appears over you. Nations will come to your light, and kings to the brightness of your dawn."

Journal Entries
OCTOBER 2006

Oct. 1st

<u>Psalm 73:23-26</u>: "Yet I am always with you, you hold me by my right hand. You guide me with your counsel, and afterward you will take me into glory. Whom have I but You? And earth has nothing I desire besides you. My flesh and my heart may fail, but God is the strength of my heart and my portion forever."

<u>Psalm 91:1-16</u>: (paraphrased) God is my refuge, I trust in you and I'm safe. He rescues me from hidden traps, shields you from deadly hazards. His huge outstretched arms protect you--under them you're perfectly safe. His arms fend off all harm. Fear nothing, not wild wolves in the night, not flying arrows in the day, not disease that prowls through the darkness. Even though others succumb all around, you'll stand untouched, watch it all from a distance. Yes, because God's your refuge, Evil can't get close to you, harm can't get through the door. He ordered his angels to guard you wherever you go; you'll walk unharmed among lions and snakes. "If you'll hold on to me for dear life," says God, "I'll get you out of trouble. I'll give you the best of care if you'll only get to know and trust me. Call me and I'll answer, be at your side in bad times; I'll rescue you, and then throw you a party. I'll give you a long life; give you a long drink of salvation."

8

Oct. 10th

Jeremiah 17:7-8: "Blessed is the man who trusts in The Lord, whose confidence is in Him. He will be like a tree planted by the water that sends out its roots by the stream. It does not fear when heat comes; its leaves are always green. It has no worries in a year of drought and never fails to bear fruit."

DECEMBER 2006

Dec. 2nd

I was lying in our bed watching television, while my husband, Mike, was watching television in the living room. Yes, we like to watch different programs sometimes. Anyways, I'm not sure how or why, but all of a sudden I felt a lump in my right breast. It hadn't been there the day before. It was like it suddenly appeared. It startled me. I called my husband into the bedroom and asked him to look at it.

He was concerned and said I should call the advice nurse and see what she says. I said I would call on Monday morning. Pretty soon I hear him on the phone talking to someone in the next room. Then, he walks into our bedroom and hands me the phone. He says it is the advice nurse and that I need to talk to her. So I did.

She asked me if it was reddened at all. I hadn't even noticed. So I looked and sure enough, it was red and sore. She said I needed to go to the emergency room since it was after clinic hours. She said the infection was too close to my heart and that I needed it looked at.

So, off we went to the local emergency room. They said, yes, it was infected and gave me antibiotics and told me to follow up with my doctor. They weren't too concerned about it.

Dec. 3rd

This morning I was trying to get ready for church, but I was feeling so emotional. I do not like to be emotional in front of other people; I've always felt that was a weakness on my part. Not for anyone else though, only for me. So I told Mike that I couldn't go to church that day. He understood and went on without me.

I just had this feeling that this lump was going to be a bigger deal than all the other lumps. I was looking at myself in the mirror in the bathroom and asked the question; "So, what's in my future?"

I'll never forget that moment. Loud and clear and instantaneous, I heard a reply. *God is in your future!* It was so awesome. I felt peace in that moment that no matter what was to come I knew my God would always be with me.

A friend from church shared this scripture with me that same day. Proverbs 14:4: "Where there are no oxen, the stall is clean. But strength comes from the ox."

In other words, when there are no oxen (or troubles) everything is clean and orderly. But, when there are oxen (trials, tribulations), things get messy. Strength comes out of the mess. And there is an abundant harvest and gain that goes along with it. Things might get messy here in my life and my family's life very soon, but I prayed God would use it to bring about a great harvest in all of our lives.

Dec. 4th

Psalm 121:1-8: "I lift my eyes to the hills—where does my help come from? My help comes from The Lord, the maker of heaven and earth. He will not let your foot slip—He who watches over you will not slumber; indeed, He who watches over Israel will neither slumber nor sleep. The Lord watches over you. The Lord is your shade at your right hand; the sun will not harm you by day, nor the moon by night. The Lord will keep you from all harm—He will watch over your coming and going both now and forevermore."

1 John: 4:18: "There is no fear in love. But perfect love drives out fear, because fear has to do with punishment."

It's as if The Lord was trying to prepare my heart for what was to come.

Dec. 5ᵗʰ

Psalm 124:7-8: "We have escaped like a bird out of the fowler's snare; the snare has been broken, and we have escaped. Our help is in the name of The Lord, the Maker of heaven and earth"

Dec. 6ᵗʰ

I went in for a mammogram.

Dec. 7ᵗʰ

Psalm 125:1-2: "Those who trust in The Lord are like Mt. Zion, which cannot be shaken but endures forever. As the mountains surround Jerusalem, so The Lord surrounds his people both now and forevermore."

Psalm 126: 5-6: "Those who sow in tears will reap with songs of joy. He, who goes out weeping, carrying seed to sow, will return with songs of joy carrying sheaves with him."

Dec. 8th

I saw my doctor to discuss my mammogram. My husband went with me to the appointment. My doctor, God bless him, said the mammogram came back fine, nothing to worry about. I said I would like to get a breast biopsy.

My doctor asked why, when everything looked fine. I must add here, my husband confessed later, that he wanted to give him 5 reasons why….his five fingers formed in a fist! But he stayed calm and let me do the talking! I told my doctor I would feel better getting it checked out. He agreed although he didn't really think it was necessary.

Dec. 13th

Proverbs 29:25 "Fear of man will prove to be a snare, but whoever trusts in The Lord will be kept safe."

Psalm 130: 5-6 "I wait for The Lord, my soul waits and in His word I put my hope. My soul waits for The Lord more than watchmen wait for the morning, more than watchmen wait for the morning."

Nahum 1:7 "The Lord is good, a refuge in times of trouble. He cares for those who trust in him."

Dec. 15th

I went to the surgeon, who has performed several of my former breast biopsies and knows me very well. He told me that he was sure it was nothing. He had never seen cancer from a lump such as this. He offered me three choices. We could do nothing and watch it. We could do a needle biopsy. Or, we could remove the lump and send it to pathology for testing. I chose to remove it. I was scheduled for an in office procedure to remove the lump the following week.

Dec. 19th

Zephaniah 3: 17: "The Lord your God is with you, He is mighty to save. He will take great delight in you. He will quiet you with His love, He will rejoice over you with singing."

Psalm 138:7-8: "Though I walk in the midst of trouble, you preserve my life; you stretch out your hand against the anger of my foes, with your right hand you save me. The Lord will fulfill His purpose for me; your love, O Lord, endures forever—do not abandon the works of your hands."

Dec. 21st

Revelation 12:11: "They overcame him (the accuser of the brethren) by the blood of the Lamb and the word of their testimony; they did not love their lives so much as to shrink from death."

Dec. 27th

<u>Psalm 146:5-6</u>: "Blessed is he whose help is the God of Jacob, whose hope is in The Lord his God the maker of heaven and earth, the sea and everything in them—The Lord, who remains faithful forever."

Dec. 28th

<u>Psalm 147:11</u>: "The Lord delights in those who fear Him, who put their hope in His unfailing love."

—————————————

So, I waited. I waited to hear the results. And then I waited some more. Waiting is so long when you're waiting for the results to see if you have cancer or not. The thing is, I already knew deep down in my heart, that it was cancer. God was gracious to me to tell me first. He has done that for me in other tragic circumstances in my life, like knowing before my sister committed suicide that someone close to me was going to die. And then, when my mother was extremely sick and went into the hospital, He told me I was going to lose her. She died four days later.

Dec. 29th

I worked at the hospital in the coffee shop where my surgeon's office was. It had been nine days since the surgery. I was tired of waiting. My husband came by the coffee shop after work, although I was not expecting him to. After I got off work, he and I headed up to the doctor's office together. I'm so glad my husband came by that day; otherwise I would have heard the news alone.

When we got to the clinic, they all knew who I was as they all got coffee at the coffee shop where I worked. I told them I had not heard any news yet and was wondering if my doctor was in. It was at the end of the day. So they put us in a room to wait for my doctor.

My husband and I are sitting in the room, waiting, when all of a sudden, in the hallway we hear my doctor. He is very angry. He is saying that he can't believe it took that long to get the results back to him. My doctor doesn't get angry. My husband and I just look at each other.

We know this can't be good. My doctor comes in the room and gives us the news. It's cancer. The lump was not cancerous; the cancer was hidden in the breast tissue down underneath the lump, where the mammogram could not find it. He said he had never seen anything like this before.

I want to add here that I felt the lump was like an "X" that marked the spot where the cancer was. Had there been no lump, the cancer would not have been found, until maybe it was too late.

All of this came on a Friday afternoon, the weekend of New Years Eve. There wasn't much to do about anything until the following week when I would come back and discuss my options with my doctor then.

The tough part here was not only was I just diagnosed with breast cancer, but that very weekend, we were taking my baby to Pullman to start college. Why oh why do these things have to come in clumps? Somehow I got through that weekend, with cancer and all that it entailed constantly on my mind and saying good-bye to my youngest son.

When we got home after being diagnosed we had the difficult task of telling our kids the news. You don't realize how hard it is to tell those you love that you have cancer, until you have to do it. My poor husband couldn't do it. I had to be the one to tell them. Emotionally I hold it together a little better, until I'm alone.

Then I let it all out. So that's what I did that weekend, emotionally held it all together, through telling our children and my husband's parents, and saying good-bye to our youngest son.

JANUARY 2007

Jan. 3rd

(My first day alone after being diagnosed) What an AWESOME time with the Lord today!! I was feeling so emotional and messed up. I put in my Daryl Evans Freedom CD and just sat on the floor in the living room with the music turned up loud. I worshiped! Oh how I needed it. The Lord has reminded me how important worship is. It is my strength and my joy. It's what will get me through all of this.

Habakkuk 3:17-19: "Though the cherry trees don't blossom and the strawberries don't ripen. Though the apples are worm-eaten and the wheat fields stunted, though the sheep pens are sheep less and the cattle barns empty, I'm singing joyful praises to God. I'm turning cart wheels of joy to my Savior God, counting on God's rule to prevail; I take heart and gain strength. I run like a deer. I feel like I'm king of the mountain!" (The Message Version)

Mike had taped this verse on the bathroom mirror for me the weekend before. Psalms 32:7: "You are my hiding place! You keep me safe from trouble! You surround me with songs sung by those who praise you because you save your people."

I had my doctor appointment on Jan. 3rd to discuss my options in dealing with breast cancer. My doctor told my husband and me that he would like to do a lumpectomy. This is where he removes more breast tissue to see how far the cancer has spread. This is also where we find out what stage the cancer is.

We discussed the different options that we would be able to choose from, if necessary. There is chemo, radiation, and hormone treatment, all depending on how advanced the cancer is. There is also mastectomy. When I heard the word mastectomy, in my mind I am screaming, *No!* Mike asked the doctor about bilateral mastectomy, taking my risk of getting breast cancer again down to zero. Again, on the inside, I am yelling and screaming, *No way!* On the outside, I remain calm.

After my doctor appointment, I began to do research on-line to find out about all the different treatments and how they would affect me. The more I researched, the more I began to think that a mastectomy was the way I wanted to go. There are so many side affects from radiation and the hormone treatment. Radiation can burn the skin, especially with fair skinned people like me. It can also cause cancer in itself. Hormone treatment, Tamoxifen to be specific, causes your body to go into menopause. The breast cancer I was diagnosed with was sensitive to estrogen. So the idea behind it is to cause the body to not produce any so cancer won't come back. So Mike and I discussed it and he said he would support me in any decision I made.

I remember when I had told one of my sons, Isaiah, about the cancer, he calmly said to me, "Just cut them both off." He has always been my black-and-white son. There is no gray. This is what you need to do, just do it.

My response was that we'd cross that bridge if we came to it, but still thinking that it would be a radical move. Now I think he was being prophetic.

20

Jan. 4th

Psalm 3:3: "But you are a shield around me, O Lord. You bestow glory on me and lift up my head."

Psalm 4: 6-8: " ♪(song) I will rejoice in you and be glad, I will extol your love more than wine. More than when the grain and new wine abound, you have put gladness in my heart. So lift up the light of thy countenance upon me oh Lord. Draw me after you and let us run together, I will rejoice in you and be glad. ♪ I will lie down and sleep in peace, for you alone, O Lord makes me dwell in safety."

Jan 5th

Psalm 5:11-12: "But let all who take refuge in you be glad; let them ever sing for joy. Spread your protection over them, that those who love your name may rejoice in you. For surely, O Lord, you bless the righteous, you surround them with your favor as with a shield."

Jan. 7th

Genesis 15:1:   After this the word of the Lord came to Abram in a vision: "Do not be afraid, Abram. I am your shield, your very great reward!"

Matthew 5:29-30: (paraphrased) It is better to cut off one part of your body than for your whole body to be thrown into hell. *(Considering a mastectomy, hell could be cancer and my whole body being consumed by it)*

Psalm 7:10: "My shield is God Most High, who saves the upright in heart."

Jan 8th

Proverbs 2:7-8: "He holds victory in store for the upright; He is a shield to those whose walk is blameless. For He guards the course of the just and protects the way of his faithful ones."

Jan. 9th

Psalm 9:9-11:   "The Lord is a refuge for the oppressed, a stronghold in times of trouble. Those who know your name will trust in you, for you, Lord, have never forsaken those who seek you. Sing praises to the Lord, enthroned in Zion, proclaim among the nations what He has done (for you)."

Jan. 10th

Proverbs 3:3-6: "Let love and faithfulness never leave you; bind them around your neck, write them on the tablet of your heart. Then you will win favor and a good name in the sight of God and man. Trust in The Lord with all your heart and lean not on your own understanding. In all your ways acknowledge Him, and He will make your paths straight (or, direct your paths)"

Jan. 11th

I went in for my lumpectomy. More waiting for results to see how advanced the cancer was.

Jan. 15th

Psalm 13:1-6: "...How long must I wrestle with my thoughts and every day have sorrow in my heart? How long will my enemy triumph over me? ...But I trust in your unfailing love; my heart rejoices in your salvation. I will sing to The Lord, for He has been good to me."

Jan. 16th

Psalm 14:7: "Oh that salvation for Israel would come out of Zion! When The Lord restores the fortunes of His people, let Jacob rejoice and Israel be glad!"

Matthew 11:28-30: "Come to me, all you who are weary and burdened, and I will give you rest. Take my yoke upon you and learn from me, for I am gentle and humble in heart, and you will find rest for your souls. For my yoke is easy and my burden is light."

I had a dear friend that I had not seen for awhile as she had moved away. The Lord kept bringing her to my mind. I felt like I was supposed to talk to her, but I wasn't sure why. Then one Sunday, there she was in church, visiting with family. So I went up to her and told her that I had been diagnosed with breast cancer. She informed me that she also had been diagnosed with it and had a mastectomy. I did not know this about her. At that time, I didn't know anyone I could talk to about it. The women that I knew that had been diagnosed with breast cancer had all died from it.

We gave each other our email addresses so we could stay in touch. One of the verses she shared with me in those emails was: Deuteronomy 20:3-4: "Listen to me, all you men of Israel! Don't be afraid as you go out to fight today! For The Lord your God is going with you! He will fight for you against your enemies, and He will give you the victory!"

Her emails to me proved to be a life line in my times of fear, depression, and uncertainty. She shared a lot of scripture with me to encourage me and shared her story as well. She had kept a journal of her journey through breast cancer, which she shared with me. This gave me some insight as to what I might expect along my own journey. I thank God for her as she was such an inspiration and encourager to me through this difficult time.

Jan. 17th

Proverbs 3:24-26: "You will not be afraid when you lie down; your sleep will be sweet. Have no fear of sudden disaster for The Lord will be your confidence and will keep your foot from being snared."

Jan. 18th

Psalm 16:1-2: "Keep me safe, O God, for in you I take refuge. I said to The Lord, 'You are my Lord; apart from you I have no good thing.' (Verses 5-8) Lord, you have assigned me my portion and my cup; you have made my lot secure. The boundary lines have fallen for me in pleasant places; surely I have a delightful inheritance. I will praise The Lord, who counsels me; even at night my heart instructs me. I have set The Lord always before me. Because He is at my right hand I will not be shaken."

Jan. 19th

I had my follow-up appointment from the lumpectomy. My husband went to *every* appointment I had. He was always there for me, supporting me and encouraging me. I really love him for that. I saw some other women going through breast cancer alone, even though they were married.

The doctor told us that the lumpectomy revealed that there was no more cancer!!! That was wonderful news to our ears! But, he still wanted me to do radiation treatments and have me take the hormone, Tamoxifen. He said he was not worried about the breast that had cancer in it, but the other breast. He stated mastectomy was not necessary because the cancer was caught so early, at a stage 0. Also, chemotherapy wouldn't be needed as the cancer had not spread to the lymph nodes.

When I told my doctor that I was leaning toward a bilateral mastectomy, he got really stressed out. He stated that I didn't need to go that radical. Because the cancer was caught so early and that it hadn't spread, the radiation and hormone treatment would be sufficient enough. The poor man! He had never had a patient that wanted to go this route. He told me not to make any final decisions until after I saw the oncologist doctors. I agreed and got set up with appointments.

I think up until this point, I was in denial, like this isn't really happening to me. With my doctor insisting that I do radiation and hormone treatment, I began to realize this is serious. I also need to add here, that up until now, all the women I knew that had been diagnosed with breast cancer (and there were several) had died from it. So, my thought was that this was a death sentence for me. There was not much hope of survival.

This was also the time that once word got out that I had breast cancer, women began to come out of the woodwork that also had breast cancer, and survived it! Remember I worked in the coffee shop at the hospital. Everyone knew me and I could not hide, which is my tendency when I am hurting. Women were constantly coming up to me and encouraging me, telling me their stories of survival of breast cancer. At church, I was prayed for and loved on. Never had I felt such love poured out on me. God revealed himself to me in ways I could never had imagined.

Jan. 20th

Psalm 18:1-6: "I love You O Lord my strength. The Lord is my rock, my fortress and my deliverer. My God is my Rock, in whom I take refuge. He is my shield and the horn of my salvation, my stronghold. I call to The Lord, who is worthy of praise and I am saved from my enemies. The cords of death entangled me; the torrents of destruction overwhelmed me. The cords of the grave coiled around me, the snares of death confronted me. In my distress, I called to The Lord; I cried to my God for help. From His temple He heard my voice, my cry came before Him, into His ears."

Jan. 22

I went to the breast cancer support group that the hospital offered once a month. I sat in a large room surrounded by women, all going through different stages of breast cancer. We went around the room and shared our name and a little information about ourselves. I was so encouraged to hear these women share their stories! I really needed to hear them.

When it came to my turn, I shared how all the women I had known with breast cancer had died. The other women in the group said that I should not use the "D" word. But, I told them, how encouraged I was to hear all these stories of survival. It was exactly what I needed to hear. It gave me hope.

Jan. 24th

Psalm 20:1-9: "May The Lord answer you when you are in distress. May the name of The God of Jacob protect you. May He send you help from the sanctuary and grant you support from Zion. May He remember all your sacrifices and accept your burnt offerings. May He give you the desire of your heart and make all your plans succeed. We will shout for joy when you are victorious and will lift up our banners in The Name of God. May The Lord grant all your requests. Now I know that The Lord saves his anointed; he answers him from His holy heaven with the saving power of His right hand. Some trust in chariots and some in horses, but we trust in the name of The Lord our God! They are brought to their knees and fall, but we rise up and stand firm. O Lord, save the King! Answer us when we call!"

Jan. 27th

Matthew 18:18-19: "I tell you the truth, whatever you bind on earth will be bound in heaven, and whatever you loose on earth will be loosed in heaven. Again, I tell you that if two of you on earth agree about anything you ask for, it will be done for you by my Father in heaven. For where two or three come together in my name, there am I with them."

Psalm 23 (The Message) God, my Shepherd! I don't need a thing. You have bedded me down in lush meadows; you find me quiet pools to drink from. True to your word, you let me catch my breath and send me in the right direction. Even when the way goes through Death Valley, I'm not afraid when you walk at my side. Your trusty shepherd's crook makes me feel secure. You serve me a six-course dinner right in front of my enemies. You revive my drooping head; my cup brims with blessing. Your beauty and love chase after me every day of my life. I'm back home in the house of God for the rest of my life."

Psalm 25:1-15: "To you O Lord, I lift up my soul; in you I trust, O my God. Do not let me be put to shame, nor let my enemies triumph over me. No one whose hope is in you will ever be put to shame….Show me your ways, O Lord, teach me your paths, guide me in your truth and teach me, for you are God, my Savior. And my hope is in you all day long! Remember O Lord, your great mercy and love, for they are from old. Remember not the sins of my youth and my rebellious ways, according to your love remember, for you are good, O Lord…."

Jan. 30th

I went to see an oncologist to discuss radiation treatments. He explained what happens during these treatments and how long they last. He was ready for me to begin right away. I was thinking, *Hold on buddy! I am not ready to commit to anything yet.* But, I calmly told him that I needed time to think about what I was going to do. I told him I would call later to set up appointments, if this was the route I chose to take.

FEBRUARY 2007

Feb. 5th

I had an appointment with another oncologist. This one discussed breast cancer treatments with us. He asked us what we would like to do. Mike and I began to tell him that we were thinking bilateral mastectomy.

After the doctor heard what we had decided, he told us that he and his wife had discussed if she were to ever get breast cancer, that she would have a bilateral mastectomy. He told us that the different treatments of cancer cause their own problems and need their own treatments. It is a vicious cycle.

That made Mike and I feel so much better, knowing this doctor and his wife would choose the same thing. I also know he would have supported whatever treatment we had chosen and would not have told us this if we had not chosen mastectomy.

Mike and I did a lot of on-line shopping at this point. We were shopping for breasts. We would pull up photos of women (They were all faceless) that had mastectomies and discuss what we wanted me to look like. The before and after pictures gave us an idea of what I might look like after surgery. It was kind of strange to be looking at women's breasts on the computer, but it was something we could do together since we were connected in every intimate detail of the process. It was also kind of humorous. You can either laugh or cry through these things. Mike and I chose to see the humorous side. I mean how many husbands and wives get to go booby shopping?!

Feb. 6th

Psalm 30:5: "For His anger lasts only a moment, but His favor lasts a lifetime. Weeping may remain for a night, but rejoicing comes in the morning. (Vs 11) You turned my wailing into dancing, you removed my sackcloth and clothed me with joy!"

Psalm 28:6-7: "Praise be to The Lord for He has heard my cry for mercy. The Lord is my strength and my shield, my heart leaps for joy and I will give thanks to Him in song."

Psalm 27:13-14: "I am still confident of this: I will see the goodness of The Lord in the land of the living. Wait for the Lord; be strong and take heart and wait for the Lord."

Psalm 27:1: "The Lord is my light and my salvation--whom shall I fear? The Lord is the stronghold of my life—of whom shall I be afraid?"

Psalm 31: 14-15: "My times are in your hands; deliver me from my enemies and from those who pursue me. Let your face shine on your servant; save me in your unfailing love."

Feb. 9th

The Lord shared with me last night that He is "expanding" my heart like the expanders will do to my breasts when I have reconstruction. So I looked up the definition of expand. I probably should add here that I like to look up words in the dictionary to expound on their meanings. I have always loved words, and to look up what they mean brings so much more into the picture.

Expand: To make or become larger, to increase in bulk or importance. To unfold or spread out; to give a fuller account of, to write out in full (what is condensed or abbreviated), to become genial, to throw off ones reserve. (Expander)

God is expanding my heart by filling it more and more with His love for me. He keeps showing me how much He loves me through other people, especially since I was diagnosed with cancer. (Darrell Evans song—"My heart gets bigger for you, Lord")

Feb. 12th

Exodus 33:11, 12-19: "The Lord would speak to Moses face to face as as a man speaks with his friend"…..Moses said, "You have said 'I know you by name and you have found favor with me.' If you are pleased with me, teach me your ways so I may know you and continue to find favor with you. Remember that this nation is your people." The Lord replied, "My presence will go with you and I will give you rest." Then Moses said to Him, "If your Presence does not go with us, do not send us up from here. How will anyone know that you are pleased with me and with your people unless you go with us? What else will distinguish me and your people from all the other people on the face of the earth?" And The Lord said to Moses, "I will do the very thing you have asked, because I am pleased with you and I know you by name." Then Moses said, "Now show me your glory" (And He did!)

Psalm 33:18-22: "But the eyes of The Lord are on those who fear him, on those whose hope is in His unfailing love, to deliver them from death and keep them alive in famine. We wait in hope for the Lord; He is our help and our shield. In Him our hearts rejoice, for we trust in His Holy name. May your unfailing love rest upon us, O Lord, even as we put our hope in you."

Feb. 13ᵗʰ

Psalm 34:4: "I sought The Lord and He answered me; He delivered me from all my fears. Those who look to Him are radiant".....vs 7-8: "The angel of The Lord encamps around those who fear Him, and He delivers them. Taste and see that The Lord is good, blessed is the man who takes refuge in Him."

Feb. 15ᵗʰ

Psalm 35: 1-3: "Contend (to fight; especially in competition or against difficulties), O Lord, with those who contend with me; fight against those who fight against me. Take up shield and buckler; arise and come to my aid. Brandish spear and javelin against those who pursue me. Say to my soul, "I am your salvation!"

Feb 19th

Psalm 37:3-7: "Trust in The Lord and do good; dwell in the land and enjoy safe pasture. Delight yourself in The Lord and He will give you the desires of your heart. Commit your way to The Lord, trust in Him and He will do this; He will make your righteousness shine like the dawn, the justice of your cause like the noonday sun. Be still before The Lord and wait patiently for Him."

Mark 5:24-29: "A large crowd followed and pressed around Him. And a woman was there who had been subject to bleeding for twelve years. She had suffered a great deal under the care of many doctors and had spent all she had, yet instead of getting better she grew worse. When she touched Jesus cloak, she was healed and freed from her suffering, because of her faith in Jesus."

I have 3 choices in dealing with this breast cancer:

(1) <u>Do absolutely nothing</u> and be at the mercy of the cancer coming back or not (there is no mercy in cancer)
(2) <u>Do the man-made treatments</u> and be at the mercy of man and pay all the money that goes with it and experience all the side effects that go along with them.
(3) <u>Remove both breasts</u> and be at the mercy of God

February 21ˢᵗ

I had another doctor appointment. The funny thing about this was the night before I had gotten no sleep, as we had a cat howling outside our window ALL night long!! I had to get up and go to work the next morning and boy, was I tired!!! This appointment was when we were supposed to tell my doctor what treatments we had decided upon. We shared with the doctor that I had been up all night with a crazy howling cat.

When I told my doctor that I wanted to pursue the bilateral mastectomy, he told me I needed to go home and get some sleep and think about my decision some more. He just didn't want me to make any rash decisions based on no sleep. He was having a hard time with my decision. I actually felt sorry for him as he was stressed out and really wanted me to be sure of what I wanted to do. I told him I was pretty sure, but we would talk again at my next appointment.

Feb 26ᵗʰ

Psalm 42:1-2: "As the deer pants for streams of water, so my soul pants for you, O God, for the living God. When can I go and meet with God? (Vs 8) By day The Lord directs His love, at night His song is with me—a prayer to The God of my life."

Feb. 27ᵗʰ

Psalm 43:5: "Why are you downcast, O my soul? Why so disturbed within me? Put your hope in God, for I will yet praise Him, my savior and my God!"

I've been feeling downcast lately. The surgery looms over me. The wait seems long. I try to prepare myself mentally for it, but I don't think I can really. Not until it happens can I really go through it. I wouldn't say I'm scared, but I am feeling anxious and a bit nervous.

It's going to be a BIG change in my life. Am I ready? How can I be? I can only guess at what it will be like. I'm sad it has to be this way, but at the same time, thankful. Thankful it was caught early, thankful I have a choice at all, and thankful I will be able to encourage other women.

There is no way to ever know if my decision is the absolute right one. There is no way to know if cancer would come back or how bad it would be if it did. No way to know if I really needed to get a bilateral mastectomy. I put my hope and trust in you, my God. You are my light and my salvation, my shield and my fortress. I pray this surgery is not in vain, but your will for my life. I can get through anything if I know it's your will and that you are with me.

(Song) ♪ Be bold; be strong, for The Lord Your God is with you. I am not afraid; I am not dismayed, for I'm walking in faith and victory. For The Lord my God is with me!! ♪

(A song The Lord gave me a few years ago) ♪I want to be what You want me to be. I want to know your will, I want to hear your voice, I want a faith that will move mountains! I want to be your servant, O Lord. I want to be your own. Make me, change me, shape me Lord, into what you will. I want to be what You want me to be. ♪

MARCH, 2007

March 1st

Mark 9:43-48: "If your hand caused you to sin, cut it off. It's better to enter life maimed than with 2 hands to go into hell, where the fire never goes out. And if your foot causes you to sin, cut it off. It's better to enter life crippled than to have 2 feet and be thrown into hell. And if your eye causes you to sin, pluck it out. It's better to enter the Kingdom of God with one eye than to have 2 eyes and be thrown into hell where the worm does not die and the fire is not quenched."

Again, I feel like The Lord has told me it's better to remove my breasts, than to have them and be thrown into the hell of cancer just so I could keep them.

Psalm 44:3: "It was not by their sword that they won the land, nor did their arm bring them victory. It was your right hand, your arm and the light of your face, for you loved them." (Vs 6) "I do not trust in my bow, my sword does not bring me victory, but you give us victory over our enemies, you put our adversaries to shame. In God we make our boast all day long and we will praise your name forever!!"

March 2nd

I had another doctor appointment. I reassured my doctor that the bilateral mastectomy was what I wanted to do. My surgery was finalized and I waited for a surgery date.

March 6th

Mark 12: 29-30: "The most important commandment, answered Jesus, is this; Hear, O Israel, The Lord our God, The Lord is one. Love The Lord your God with all your heart and with all your mind and with all your soul, and with all your strength. The second is this; Love your neighbor as yourself. There is no commandment greater than these." (vs. 33) "To love Him with all your heart, with all your understanding and with all your strength, to love your neighbor as yourself is more important than all burnt offerings and sacrifices.....Jesus replied after the man answered wisely—you are not far from the Kingdom of God."

Psalm 48:9: "Within your temple, O God, we meditate on your unfailing love."

Numbers 6:22-27: "The Lord said to Moses, tell Aaron and his sons, this is how you are to bless the Israelites. Say to them: 'The Lord bless you and keep you; The Lord make His face shine upon you and be gracious to you; The Lord turn His face toward you and give you peace.' So they will put my name on the Israelites and I will bless them."

March 7th

Last night when I went to bed, I was praying about getting a mastectomy. I had been feeling down and depressed, kind of detached from ever having cancer at all. Was I sure bilateral mastectomy was the right thing to do?

I felt The Lord showed me flowers and how some are pruned back after they are done blooming so they will come back even fuller and more beautiful the next time they bloom. Like my climbing Clematis. When Mike cuts it back and prunes it, it comes back prettier and fuller the next year.

The Lord said my breasts will be like that. They will be pruned back, and they will grow back fuller and more beautiful than before. And the fruit produced will be plentiful; the fruit of encouragement and hope to other women will come from it too. This surgery will not be in vain.

I got my surgery date, April 6th. That's Good Friday, the day Jesus was crucified and died; Easter weekend, when Jesus rose from the dead; the very symbol of new life. I'm having my surgery on the very weekend when death and new life took on new meaning. I know this is NOT a coincidence; this is God's way of reminding me of His promise of salvation and new life.

Just like the flowers that bloom every spring, representing life and beauty—so my surgery is new life for me and for other women, too, as God uses this to reach out to those going through breast cancer. Please Lord, I want to be what you want me to be. I want you to use me and my life to help and encourage others and to give them hope. I love you my Lord. You are my everything!

I wanted to add the reason my surgery isn't until April 6th is because my doctor will be gone the last week of March. And he didn't want to perform surgery and then leave. He wants to be here for me afterwards. Lord, I know this is you again showing me how much you love me and care about me and are taking care of me and seeing me through this.

Thank you for your everlasting love for me. I love you with all my heart!!

Psalms 50:14:   "Sacrifice thank offerings to God, fulfill your vows to the Most High, and call upon me in the day of trouble; I will deliver you and you will honor me." (Paraphrased) What I want from you is your true thanks; I want your promises fulfilled. I want you to trust me in your times of trouble, so I can rescue you, and you can give me glory. (vs. 23) "But true praise is a worthy sacrifice; this really honors me. Those who walk my paths will receive salvation from The Lord."

March 13th

<u>Psalm 56:3-4</u>: "When I am afraid, I will trust in you. In God, whose word I praise, in God I trust; I will not be afraid. What can mortal man do to me?"

March 15th

<u>Psalm 57: 2-3</u>: "I cry out to God Most High, to God, who fulfills His purpose for me. He sends from heaven and saves me, rebuking those who hotly pursue me; God sends forth His love and His faithfulness. (vs. 10) For great is your love, reaching to the heavens; your faithfulness reaches to the skies. Be exalted, O God, above the heavens; let your glory be over all the earth!"

March 18th

<u>Psalm 61</u>: "Hear my cry, O God; listen to my prayer. From the ends of the earth I call to you. I call as my heart grows faint; lead me to The Rock that is higher than I. For you have been my refuge, a strong tower against my foe. I long to dwell in your tent forever and take refuge in the shelter of your wings."

<u>Psalm 62:7</u>: "My salvation and my honor depend on God. He is my mighty rock, my refuge. Trust in Him at all times. O people, pour out your hearts to Him, for God is our refuge. (vs. 11) One thing God has spoken, two things I have heard, that You, O God, are strong and that You, O Lord, are loving. Surely you will reward each person according to what he has done."

Psalm 62:1-5: "O God, You are my God. Earnestly I seek you; my soul thirsts for you, my body longs for you in a dry and weary land where there is no water. I have seen you in the sanctuary and beheld your power and your glory. Because your love is better than life, my lips will glorify you. I will praise you as long as I live and in your name I will lift up my hands. My soul will be satisfied as with the riches of foods; with singing lips my mouth will praise you!"

March 26th

In October of 2006, I had signed up for an additional insurance coverage at work. It was optional and it covered if you were out of work due to illness. Something inside of me told me I should sign up for it. With surgery coming up, I would be missing many weeks of work. So, again the Lord showed His faithfulness to me, by offering this before I was even diagnosed with cancer.

Today I called in my claim to the insurance company and hoped and prayed for the best.

March 29th

I asked The Lord last night if He loved me, even though I knew the answer, I just needed to hear it. He answered and said to me, "Always and forever!!" How beautiful The Lord is!! Always and forever covers every moment in time—there is no lapse in His love for me and never will there be!!

APRIL 2007

April 1st

It has been six months since I started this journal. Before I was diagnosed with cancer, God encouraged me to begin to write down scripture that encouraged me. He knew, of course, what was coming and how I would need His word for strength.

Today, I was reading in Psalms 73, and I read a familiar passage. So I looked back at the beginning of this journal and sure enough, it was one of the first verses I had written in here. And, now surgery is in five days.

It's like God is bringing me back to the beginning where I started to remind me that He knew and that He is still with me and that He is still, more than ever, my refuge, my rock, and my shelter.

A friend, who had shared a verse with me when I had first been diagnosed, mailed me a card. She said she had asked God for a word for me and He gave her the same one as before, but it's still fresh and applies now more than ever. The word was <u>Proverbs 14:4</u>: "Where there is no ox, the stall is clean but much strength comes from the ox."

I was feeling a little down and sad, like, "Why me? Why do I have to go through all of this?" A good friend of mine and I had breakfast together, and she is doing very well right now with her weight, her exercising, her job, and her life. The other friend that had shared a word with me was in

Hawaii right that very minute, having a wonderful time, and here I sit and wait for a life changing surgery.

So I was feeling sorry for myself when The Lord spoke to me and said we are all in different seasons of life. The couple in Hawaii had just gone through a season of pain and suffering, and now it's their time for fun and laughter. The friend that I went to breakfast with may have a season later of suffering, but for right now, she is in a good place.

I needed to be reminded how going through all of this will bring strength. God reminded me in the verse today that came in the card in the mail.

Psalms 73:1-5: "Surely God is good to his people, Israel, to those pure in heart; but as for me, my feet had almost slipped; I had nearly lost my foothold, for I envied the arrogant when I saw the prosperity of the wicked *(or I envied those who were in "prosperous seasons")*. They have no struggles; their bodies are healthy and strong. They are free from burdens common to man; they are not plagued by human ills. (vs. 21-28) When my heart was grieved and my spirit embittered, I was senseless and ignorant. I was a brute beast before you. Yet I am always with you, you hold me by my right hand. You guide me with your counsel, and afterward you will take me into Glory. Whom have I in heaven but you? And earth has nothing I desire besides you. My flesh and my heart *(and my breasts)* may fail, but God is the strength of my heart and my portion forever!! Those who are far from you will perish; you destroy all who are unfaithful to you. But, as for me, it is good to be near God. I have made the Sovereign Lord my refuge, I will tell of all your deeds."

Thank you Father for your faithfulness!

Today God was reminding me of an encouraging word I had received in an email on January 9th, and then today I read the exact same words again:

Deuteronomy 20:3-4: "He shall say, 'Hear O Israel, today you are going into battle against your enemies. Do not be fainthearted or afraid; do not be terrified or give way to panic before them. For The Lord your God is the one who goes with you to fight for you against your enemies to give you Victory!' "

April 5th

Well, this is it, my last day on this earth with a natural and real set of breasts. Kind of a strange feeling. Tomorrow I'll go in for surgery. I'll go in with breasts, go to sleep, and wake up with none. Absolutely none.

I went up for prayer last night at church and lots of people came up to pray for me. I felt the love of God **so strongly** through them! I felt The Lord told me to love with reckless abandonment. So I looked up the word, abandon.

Abandon means to yield completely to an emotion (like love) or impulse; lacking restraint. "To restrain"—to hold back, to restrict, to put a limit on. "Reckless"—wildly impulsive. "Impulse"—a sudden inclination to act, without thought for the consequences.

It was interesting because the word restore was the word in the dictionary right above restrain. I believe God wants to restore me to what He has made me for, that is to love; without restraint, with abandonment!! And, I couldn't begin to love like that until I felt this kind of love towards me.

Going through breast cancer and now surgery of removal of my breasts, God has shown me His love for me with abandonment and without restraint, through all kinds of people—those who know Him and those who don't, people at church, at work (a lot!), people Mike knows and total strangers too!

A woman's breasts are a very personal and intimate part of a woman's body. They represent love, nurturing, sexual intimacy, and womanhood. Having them removed has affected so many people I have come in contact with. Even a hysterectomy (which I also had several years ago) isn't personal like a mastectomy.

I have seen reactions of fear and shock when I've told some people I was having them both removed. And, I've seen acceptance and agreement in others. It's such a personal decision. And yet, I know God is using this whole experience to change my heart, "expand" my love for Him and for others. To shape me into what He wants me to be. This is so much more than removal of my breasts to prevent cancer. So much more.

So, Lord, I ask you to help me love you and people with "reckless abandonment". I pray you would use this whole experience to strip away my reserves in loving you and others. Thank you Father for all that you are doing in me and what you will do through me. I love you!!! Thank you for your unfailing love for me.

Please, Lord, give me strength to get through the next 24 hours. The final count down.

April 13ᵗʰ

Well, one week ago today I was just coming out of surgery. It's been one week already. The week has gone by fast.

When we got to the hospital at 6 am, we were taken back to the waiting area by someone I knew from the coffee shop. She grabbed my hand and gave me the biggest hug. When we got to the door of my surgery prep room, the thing on the door didn't say my name; it said "Hi Sweetie." Then, another lady that worked in surgery, who also knew me from the coffee shop, came in later to hug me before I was wheeled away. A good friend from church came and prayed with me and then stayed with Mike during the surgery, along with another dear friend also from church.

I got out of surgery around 10:30 am, but not out of recovery until 3 pm. I would stop breathing and my recovery nurse (another one who knew me from the coffee shop), would say, "Martha, breathe!" That happened several times.

I finally got up to my room and Mike just sat there on my bed watching me and would touch my nose or something when I would stop breathing. Finally, I said, "Honey, you need to go home so I can rest." Several friends came up throughout the day to see me and brought flowers and a stuffed blue bear.

Friday night my blood pressure was **really** low, so they called the doctor. He said to lay me back and put my feet up and pump me full of fluids. It helped, but it stayed low. I got up to use the bathroom and never felt nauseas or dizzy—just loopy from all the drugs.

Isaiah came up Friday and Saturday, and so did a few other friends. I went home Sunday afternoon; surgery on Good Friday, home on Easter. Lots of people have called to check on me, Mike has been home to help me.

Thank you Father for your faithfulness and your love. Thank you I am recovering well.

Today I get my drain tubes pulled out---yeah! I am ready for that; and to take off this "corset!" Mike helped me to take a shower on Wednesday. We got a good look at me and my boobless state. Of course my thoughts are, *Will I ever look normal again?*

I had a couple of dreams this week. Monday I dreamt I had been taken hostage and no one knew. I tried to get people's attention to see I needed help, but no one could tell. I think I must have felt like a hostage by my body or the surgery.

Then, on Wednesday, I dreamt I was riding a bike to go get ice cream or something but, when I got there, it was totally empty so I went back, but it was getting darker and darker and no one was around. So, I pedaled faster, even though I couldn't see where I was going because I was afraid of stopping in the dark. And I got hit by a car. I spoke out in my sleep and woke Mike up. He said it sounded like I said, "Terrible". I don't know what this dream means.

Anyways, I just wanted to recap this last week for future reference. Thank you, Lord, for bringing me this far. Please continue to be with me as we move on. ♪He didn't bring us this far to leave us. He didn't teach us to swim to let us drown."♪ (Part of an old song)

April 17th

I had my drain tubes taken out last Friday and it wasn't long and I was full of fluid. My left side wiggled like a water balloon. I got very puffy and swollen. So I called the on-call doctor on Saturday (he was just a general surgeon) and he said it sounded like things were okay. They kept getting worse and my left arm tingled and kept trying to fall asleep when I lay down. So, Saturday night I stayed up until 4 a.m. because my arm bothered me so much. I took two pain pills and went to bed. I got five hours of sleep that night. Then on Sunday night, I took a Benedryl and I slept.

On Monday I went in and another doctor (not my normal surgeon) did an ultrasound on the left side to see where the expander was so she wouldn't puncture it. Then she inserted a needle and withdrew 60 ccs of liquid, which is what we were getting out of both sides plus more when Mike was emptying my drain tubes. So I was pretty full. I could feel a huge difference. She left the right side alone as it wasn't bothering me. She felt uncomfortable as I was not her patient and she doesn't know about expanders, etc. So she had called my reconstruction surgeon to find out what he wanted her to do for me. She also put me on antibiotics.

I see my reconstructive surgeon tomorrow at 5 p.m. I was surprised they never gave me a follow-up appointment with him. I had to call and make it and then they were to going to put me in with an MA and said the doctor would stop in. Well, once I told her what type of surgery I had, the appointment was changed to see my doctor and not the MA. Somewhere along the way the ball was dropped or something. I'll have to set up appointments for filling up my expanders.

I had 2 surgeons performing my mastectomy. The general surgeon did my biopsy, the lumpectomy, and then the mastectomy. The reconstructive surgeon placed the expanders during the mastectomy. He was the one I would continue to see as the reconstruction process continued.

Both of my hands and arms feel pressure and kind of tingle—worse when I lay down. A lady I know from the coffee shop, (who had double mastectomies, but done separately with no reconstruction), told me how to do an exercise that helps your body expel excess fluid build-up:

Arm Exercise: Lift both arms as high as you can over your head and squeeze your hands into fists tightly several times. Then, lower and move arms up and down, like your doing a bi-cep curl. Do this several times a day. I guess it helps the lymph nodes do their job of getting rid of excess fluid.

Deuteronomy 30:11-19: (paraphrased) "I, The Lord your God, have set before you life or death, blessing or curses. I will make you prosperous in all that you do, if you obey The Lord your God, keep His commands, and turn to The Lord your God with all your heart and with all your soul. Now what I am commanding you is not too difficult for you or beyond your reach….No, the word is very near you it is in your mouth and in your heart so you may obey it. See, I set before you today life and prosperity or death and destruction. Love The Lord your God, walk in His ways, keep His commands, decrees, and laws, and you will live and be blessed….I have set before you life and death, blessing and curses. Choose life so that you and your children may live and that you may love The Lord your God, listen to His voice and hold fast to Him. For The Lord is your life."

April 30th

Last day of April. Wow, where has the month gone?! Jami and the girls got here 10 days ago. That has been wonderful!! They are actually staying a week longer than they first planned. (Jami is my daughter and she had 2 girls at the time, ages 2 and 1)

I went to see my reconstruction surgeon on Wednesday, April 18th, and he said things look good. I got my appointments to see him every Wednesday for all of May to fill up my expanders. He will be using a little deal that moves when it gets close to the expander so he'll know where to insert to fill up the expander; like a stud finder Mike said. He also told me he put in 150 ccs of fluid in my expanders during the surgery.

I filled up with more fluid on the left side again, so I saw my surgeon again the next Wednesday, April 26th, to check it out. He said it looked okay and hated to risk infection, but to come back if it got worse. He also said the tingling in my arm and hand was because I have been sleeping with my arms bent at night on my back. The extra fluid is still there, but it hasn't gotten any worse. He also took the tape off the stitches. I have my first appointment on Wednesday to have my first filling of my expanders. Maybe he will take some of the extra fluid out then. He said sometimes when you fill the expanders it forces the extra fluid out.

Also, I have been taken Benedryl to help me sleep. One night, I think Wednesday, I had an emotional night. I couldn't sleep, so I emailed my dear friend and shared my feelings. I fell asleep on the couch from 2 a.m. to 3 a.m., and then went to bed.

The next night, I took two ducolax laxatives. Oh boy! I took them at 9 p.m. and then at 1 a.m., I woke up in a sweat and thought I was going to be sick. I thought I was going to faint and throw-up, which I didn't. I had to lie on the bathroom floor and use a wet washcloth on my face. I think I fell asleep til 6 a.m., til Mike got up for work. Then I went to bed and slept til 9 a.m.

The last couple of nights have been better. I am stiff though as I sleep on my back and don't move, so my upper arms are sore and my upper back. I took my first shower by myself a week ago.

Last Wednesday after my appointment, Jami and I visited a few people at the hospital. Then we went to Target. When I got home, I cleaned up the kitchen. That night, a friend of Jami's came over and colored her hair for her. I tried to help with the girls for a couple of hours. Needless to say, I overdid it.

 The next day, all I could do was sit around and take three naps! It's hard with the girls here. I want to do more. Jami keeps yelling at me. I haven't picked them up, but I've done everything else.

All in all, I think I'm doing well. I'm still really sore and still taking pain pills, but good. I get tired easy and need to sit down or lay back, but it's only been three weeks. I am getting there. Thank you Father for my recovery!

Journal Entries
MAY 2007

May 2ⁿᵈ

I went to my first fill-up appointment. Because I still have excess fluid on my left side, he only injected me with 60 ccs instead of a 100 ccs. Then, my general surgeon did an ultrasound to see if he could find a good place to insert a needle to drain the fluid without popping the expander, but he couldn't. There was no real significant place of just fluid. So, not to risk infection and risk of popping the expander, they left the fluid in. I was a little sore, not too bad though.

May 9ᵗʰ

I went in for my second fill-up. Still lots of excess fluid on the left side, and that side is sorer. The doctor uses his little "stud finder" and makes a mark with a pen. Then he inserts the needle into the port. He said the port is made up of silicone and when he pulls the needle out, it seals itself back up.

May 10th

When I woke up this morning, I felt like I had done a thousand or more push-ups! Very sore!

I drove for the first time since surgery—five weeks ago. I did fine. I feel more independent now knowing I can drive myself. I'll still need help with grocery shopping though, as I still can't lift anything too heavy.

Well, Jami and the girls flew home. Way too quiet around here now! She just called and yesterday's flight was rough, but they all got a good night sleep and are doing much better today. Thank you Lord!

May 11th

The right side's port is high up on my chest and it hurts really good when he puts the needle in and while he's filling it up. The left side's port is lower and it's numb there from surgery so I can't feel the needle. He put in 100ccs of fluid. Wow, I felt huge! You can really see the difference. The right side seemed sorer, maybe because it's not stretched out like the left side is from the excess fluid.

They are getting harder. Today, I am still sore, but not as bad. My doctor had told me they try to put back the amount they took off, weight wise. They just feel weird, so unnatural. Yes, I am getting bigger, but they feel so hard, like a man's chest. I know they will continue to feel hard until the silicone implants go in, probably in three months or so.

As far as going back to work, my doctor said a lot of women go back to office type work right away as they are going through the fill-up stage. But my work is very hands on and takes a lot of arm muscle. He said we'll see how I'm feeling. I know I'm not ready to go back yet. Especially after Wednesday's appointment. I was so sore! So, we'll see.

Jami called me a few minutes ago and then had to hang up. So, I called her right back to tell her some things and she said she had to go. (She was shopping) I just realized I have gotten used to having her around and talking to her again. She has her own life, she's busy, and she's back at home now. She doesn't have time to just stop everything and talk to me. I have to get used to the fact that she's not here anymore.

Lord, please help me to disconnect again. I can't keep calling her to tell her about every little thing. I need to wait for her to call me, when she has time. She's the busy one. It's just so hard as for the last three weeks she's been here and it's been wonderful. Now I have to go back to reality which is my life with no Jami and no grandbabies in it. Withdrawal is never easy or fun. I am so thankful they were here though for three whole weeks. What a blessing! Thank you Father.

As soon as I finished writing the above and was feeling sorry for myself, a friend from church called and said they would like to go out to dinner or come out and bring dinner. I told her I'd like to go out. Lord, I know what you are doing; you are reminding me I have other people in my life besides my daughter and granddaughters. Thank you. You are so faithful. I am feeling so emotional today. I keep crying. I hate that!

May 15th

I went through all my clothes (Tried on lots!), paid bills and other paper work, unloaded and loaded the dishwasher, went to town, came home, cooked dinner and cleaned up, and went back to town with Jacob, our youngest son home for a break from college.

May 16th

I had a bad night last night. I went to bed around 11 p.m. or so. I could not sleep. I overdid it yesterday. When I went to bed, my ribs hurt under my chest really bad. I couldn't go to sleep. I lay in bed and cried for whatever reason. I am so frustrated as I am still so sore. My upper arms and upper back are so sore and stiff. My left arm still tingles and bothers me. There's still lot of fluid on the left side.

If someone were to ask me if I miss my breasts, I'd say no, not really. But, why am I so emotional some days like today? I know the physical pain and soreness is taking its toll. Jami and the girls are gone, so I am alone more with no one to talk to. I could call someone, but no one I know has gone through what I'm going through. I do notice women's breasts in real life and on TV. I notice how nice and full and soft they look and how they aren't going through any pain with theirs.

Sure, I wish I didn't have mine removed, didn't have breast cancer and my life so dramatically changed. I still believe I made the right choice; but the pain and soreness and everything else that goes with having both of your breasts removed can get to you after awhile.

I have emailed my friend, who also had a mastectomy, a couple of times and asked her some questions. She has been so encouraging and helpful. But, she only had one side done and only went to a B size; whereas I had both done and am going to a C size.

I was taking Benedryl to help me sleep every night, but the last couple of nights I didn't take any. Mike and I walked Sunday and Monday and that seemed to help. But, last night at 2:30 a.m. I got up and took one and lay on the couch. I finally fell asleep around 4 a.m., and then I woke up and went to bed. I got up around 10 a.m.

I'm taking it easy today. I haven't done anything except write in here and a little reading. I feel so frustrated, I don't have anything to compare to, to know if how I'm feeling is normal or not. I did read an article in a women's breast cancer magazine about feelings after having a mastectomy. It did make me feel a little better. It's okay to be sad sometimes, like I am today. The tears keep coming—every so often—today and last night.

I know not having any money since I'm not working weighs on me too. I still don't know if I will get more money from the disability insurance or not. I called them today and they said they had received the paperwork today from the doctor's office and its being evaluated. It's in God's hands, I know. I am praying it goes through and I'll get paid for all the weeks I'm off of work. What a blessing that will be!!

Today I go in for my 3rd fill-up. I'm a little worried how I'll do with more fluid added. Will I be able to handle 100ccs? I want this process to be over, but I don't know how I'll do with every week of 100ccs being put in. I'm already tight and sore. I'm thinking of taking some money out of our trip fund to get a ½ hour massage and then go see my chiropractor. I think that would help a lot. Also, a pedicure sounds wonderful. It's no fun being poor!! I'm **Broke**, **Boobless**, and **Bottoming** out! (Means my behind has gotten bigger.)

My fill-up appointment went well. I was worried about getting filled up with 100ccs, but my doctor only put in 50ccs in each side instead. Definitely not as bad, of course, we'll see how I feel tomorrow. He said there's no recipe and we'll go with how I feel.

 He also said it's okay to cancel a fill-up if I am too sore that day. He also said to try ice on my chest for soreness and ibuprofen too. He said things are looking really well, despite the fact that I had breast reduction years ago. I think he's referring to all the scarring. He said you never know what you're going to get after a reduction and then doing a mastectomy. (P.S. I put a bag of frozen corn on my chest. It really helped with the soreness.)

May 18th

6 weeks ago today was my surgery. I would be pretty much healed up by now if I wasn't getting filled up every week. Oh well, I'll get there eventually.

<u>Psalm 115:1:</u> (song) ♪ Not to us, O Lord, not to us, but to your name be the Glory because of your love and faithfulness. ♪ (vs. 9) O house of Israel, trust in The Lord, He is your help and shield. (vs. 11) You who fear Him trust in The Lord, He is your help and shield. (vs. 12) The Lord remembers us and will bless those who fear The Lord— small and great alike. (vs. 14-18) May The Lord make you increase, both you and your children. May you be blessed by The Lord the Maker of heaven and earth...... It is not the dead who praise The Lord, those who go down to silence; it is we who extol The Lord, both now and forever more! PRAISE THE LORD!   AMEN!

May 23rd

<u>Psalm 118:4-9:</u> "Let those who fear The Lord say, 'His love endures forever.' In my anguish I cried to The Lord, and he answered me by setting me free. The Lord is with me, I will not be afraid. What can man do to me? The Lord is with me; he is my helper. I will look in triumph on my enemies. It is better to take refuge in The Lord than to trust in man. It is better to take refuge in the Lord than trust in princes....(vs. 13-16) I was pushed back and about to fall, but The Lord helped me. The Lord is my strength and my song. He has become my salvation. Shouts of joy and victory resound in the tents of the righteous. The Lord's right hand has done mighty things! The Lord's right hand is lifted high; The Lord's right hand has done mighty things."

May 24ᵗʰ

Yesterday I had my fill-up appointment. I told my doctor to put in a 100ccs again, so he did. I am so sore! This is going to take awhile to get where I need to be. He said we need to put back at least 700ccs. I am at 300ccs now. I'm not even half way yet? I'm not big, but I feel HUGE!

I won't be having my next surgery to replace the expanders with the implants until September or October. Maybe I'll get them for my birthday.

My doctor gave me a note to go back to work next Tuesday. I am looking forward to working again—on light duty.

We are going up to some friend's cabin up north this weekend for Memorial Day weekend. I am looking forward to getting out and away for a couple of days.

May 31st

Last day of May. Wow, summer is here! I had a fill-up app yesterday. I asked my doctor for less, so he put in 60ccs. I am sore, of course, but not as bad as a 100ccs would have been. He said he put in 150ccs at surgery, so now I am at a total of 520ccs. I think we're aiming for around 700ccs, so I am almost there.

Poor Mike, he's afraid I won't be as big as I was before. He's so funny, on the one hand he's like—go ahead, take them off if it will save my wife's life. But, if you're putting them back, make sure they're big.

I still haven't gone back to work as the note my doctor wrote wasn't detailed enough for Human Resources. Frustrating, as I should have worked Tuesday and yesterday. Not Thursdays though, as I am too sore. He's supposed to fax another note in today so hopefully I can work tomorrow.

I have an interview today for a job with Admitting. It's a no-guarantee-hours job. I would still work at the coffee shop and work on my off hours, if I get the job. It will be good to learn another skill and it will help me get another job someday, if I get it, that is. We'll see.

We had a wonderful relaxing weekend with our friends. We sat around in our pjs, drank coffee, talked, watched a couple of movies and ate good food. I built a fire on Sunday for us girls to enjoy while both Mike's went for a boat ride. I wanted to go out on the boat, but it was rainy and cold. Another time......

I was feeling discouraged tonight—and FAT! It takes so long to get where you want to be, in losing weight and in the right size of breasts! The process seems so long, every

Wednesday getting more fluid added and then being sore and in pain. I am on the right track of trying to eat better and I have lost 4 lbs. I am at least half ways there to the right breast size, so I am getting there –SLOWLY!

As I was sitting there feeling discouraged, I felt The Lord say, "Though the going is slow, you must keep going". He's absolutely right! Never give up even though it may take awhile to get there. I feel emotional tonight, on the verge of tears—again.

I do get to go back to work tomorrow—finally! I just pray it goes well. I am looking forward to seeing everyone again. It gets lonely staying at home all day by myself with no one to talk to.

The job in admitting won't work out. They would have needed me more available than I can be working at the coffee shop. Also, it would be in the ED a lot, and I don't know if I could handle that. Maybe I don't give myself enough credit….. I'll keep looking….

JUNE, 2007

June 1st

Psalm 119:49-50: "Remember your (The Lord's) word to your servant, for you have given me hope. My comfort in my suffering is this: Your promise preserves my life. (vs57) You are my portion, O Lord; I have promised to obey your words. I have sought your face with all my heart; be gracious to me according to your promise."

Proverbs 16:1-3: "To man belongs the plans of the heart, but from The Lord comes the reply of the tongue. All man's ways seem innocent to him, but motives are weighed by The Lord. Commit to The Lord whatever you do, and your plans will succeed." (Commit—to entrust for safe keeping—place in God's hands) (vs. 9)"In his heart a man plans his course, but The Lord determines his steps."

June 2ⁿᵈ

Psalm 119: 67-68: "Before I was afflicted I went astray, but now I obey your word. You are good and what you do is good; teach me your decrees. (vs71) It was good for me to be afflicted so I might learn your decrees. (vs75) I know, O Lord that your laws are righteous and in your faithfulness you have afflicted me. **May your unfailing love be my comfort**, according to your promise to your servant. Let your compassion come to me that I may live, for your law is my delight."

Proverbs 16:4: "The Lord works out everything for his own ends—even the wicked for a day of disaster."

June 5ᵗʰ

Psalm 119:88-92: "Preserve my life according to your love, and I will obey the statutes of your mouth. Your word, O Lord, is eternal; it stands firm in the heavens. Your faithfulness continues through all generations, you established the earth, and it endures. Your laws continue to this day, for all things serve you. If your law had not been my delight, I would have perished in my affliction."

June 7

Well, I had my appointment yesterday. My doctor only put in 60ccs. I think that brings me up to 580ccs. I'm sore. I can't even imagine them stretching anymore. They are so hard! I am not working today, which is a good thing. My doctor said it would be good if I did 100ccs next week. I don't know though, I really dread doing that much. Especially having my appointment after I've worked and I'm already sore from working.

He also said that my next surgery should be like six weeks after I reach the right size. He said he likes to have three months between surgeries, and that should be July sometime. But, my fill-up apps have stretched out so far, that it probably won't be until August. But that's two months sooner than I thought. So, surgery should be in August and he said I'd probably need one to two weeks off. I know one of the girls working in the coffee shop has a week off the last week of August and the other girl is only working until the end of August, as she is quitting. So, this could be interesting.

June 8

Yesterday was an emotional day for me. I was sore from my fill-up app, for one thing. Mike had to work over till 11:30 pm. He worked a double! Then at night, I just felt really down.

I am eating too much—stress eating. I feel so fat and very undesirable, mostly because my boobies are so hard. They are not feminine at all and are uncomfortable. I don't know, some days I just feel down, ya know.

I'm ready to be done with my fill-ups. I'm ready for my implants, but that's still two months away. I think this is just all wearing on me—physically and emotionally. So, I am eating more, which makes me fatter and that does not help!! I want to be losing weight! I need, really need, to be at least exercising more. That would help me, I know.

Of course, I went back to work this week, so that has made me more tired. I was so tired yesterday, all day, too. I am glad to be back to work though, but it does tire me out more than when I wasn't working. It's good for me to get out and get my mind off of me! I just pray that I can do four hours a day next week, without wearing myself out.

June 14

Well, another fill-up appointment behind me. I got 100ccs yesterday. Needless to say, very sore! I am very glad I'm not working today. I am closing tomorrow, hopefully that goes well. Work this week went well though. I did ask if I could change my hours so I don't work by myself so long and they agreed to changing them a bit. It helps.

I won't be having another appointment with my doctor until July 11th. I am now at 680ccs. He wants me to just wait now and let things soften up a bit. He said he might put a little more in at my next appointment. I should also find out then when my next surgery will be, maybe end of July or 1st of August. We'll see.

June 29

Let's see, since I wrote in here last, I am back to work my regular hours now. I am doing much better since I haven't had a fill-up for 2 weeks. Still wake up a lot in the night since I can only sleep on my back. Oh, how I long to sleep on my side.

Psalm 147: 10-11: "His pleasure is not in the strength of the horse, nor his delight in the legs of a man; The Lord delights in those who fear Him, who put their hope in His unfailing love."

Journal Entries
JULY, 2007

July 1st

4 a.m.—I've been awake since around 1:30 a.m. I can't sleep! So I got out of bed and lay on the couch. I felt like something might be bothering me, so I began to pray about it. I asked The Lord what was wrong with me. And I believe He answered me.

I began to cry as I realized I have been feeling trapped, in a way. Trapped in the sense that, for one thing, my body has limits since my surgery. I can only sleep on my back, I hurt a lot and my chest is so hard and unmovable! I feel like this whole year I have been "trapped" in my home. With my surgeries, recovering time, and not making very much money since I've missed so much work, I can't really go anywhere or do anything. I feel like it's been forever since Mike and I did anything fun.

The highlight of this week was when Mike and I drove around Longview, checking out my brother and sister-in-law's new house out on 50th. It was a beautiful day. Then we walked a couple sections of the lake.

As I was praying, I kept thinking of how I need a change of scenery. I feel like all I have done so far this year is stare at my four walls.

I was thinking, *I need a vacation!* But, we really don't have the time, as all my time off has been connected with my surgeries. We don't have the money either to go on any trips—like to Hawaii. So, what can I do to get a change of scenery? Then, The Lord showed me something. There are lots of places to go to that are close by to get away for the day. That's why Mike goes fishing, hiking, bike riding, etc. They are like mini vacations. You get outdoors and see God's creation. You get revived and refreshed.

I was just reminded (in my spirit) of how when I had my break down in 1992, I realized we had been doing nothing as a family together, except the daily grind of life. That is when Mike started the family fund and we began to do family outings—like bike riding, camping, and hiking. We had a lot of fun. It's fifteen years later now, and I've had another major development in my life. In 1992 I had a nervous breakdown and learned to relax more and spend time doing fun things with my family. This year I was diagnosed with breast cancer—a life changing diagnosis.

So far this year, I've had two surgeries, with another one coming probably in a few weeks. Then another smaller procedure to reconstruct nipples still needs to be done. It seems all I've done this year is stare at the four walls of my house. It's getting depressing. So, I feel The Lord is trying to tell me to get up and get out of this house.

The major part of my recovery is behind me now. Today, when Mike and I walked the lake, he said he wants to start hiking more, maybe with someone from church, as he knows I haven't wanted to. Well, I want to change that. I am out of shape, so I need to start slow, but as of **now**, I want to start getting out and doing more fun things. A lot of them don't cost anything, except maybe some gas to get there. I am going to make a list and talk to Mike about it. I'm sure he will be ecstatic.

My prayer Lord is that you will restore and revive my love and passion I had for the outdoors when I was a kid. I know it's in me still, just buried under older age, life, physical pains, cares of the world, etc. Please Lord, bring it back, and let it grow. I want to enjoy life, not just exist. I love your creation, I always have. That's why I love to go to Hawaii and to the beach, and what I loved about my paper route—getting outside everyday and seeing God's creation, like the mountains, the scenery, etc.

It's almost five a.m. I need sleep. Thank you Father for revealing this to me. I feel better now, more alive. I may be almost fifty years old, my joints hurt more, and I ache all over more, but so what? It's better to hurt and be active and happy than sitting around the house and doing and seeing the same things day in and day out.

July 4th

Mike and I went to Fort Stevens and rode bikes for an hour. It felt good to be out and doing something fun! It was windy, but otherwise a beautiful day. Then, we went to Cannon Beach for lunch. It was a nice day.

July 7th

Psalms 5: 11-12: "But let all who take refuge in you be glad; let them ever sing for joy. Spread your protection over them that those who love your name may rejoice in you. For surely, O Lord, you bless the righteous, you surround them with your favor as with a shield."

I am so discouraged with my weight right now. I am at the heaviest I've been for awhile. I try to do well, and then I do bad; back and forth. This has been a very stressful year and I know that is probably the main reason. But I need to start on the road to recovery. I want to lose 25 to 30 lbs; get my second surgery, in which I'll feel more normal. Please Lord help me to get out of this slump and get on the right road again. Please help me to lose this weight. I can't do it alone.

July 11th

Well, I had my last fill-up appointment today, and my doctor did a grand finale of 100 ccs. He said it's better to over expand, as it looks better, more settled and relaxed. So, I won't be working tomorrow. My next surgery to replace my expanders with silicone is scheduled for July 27th. Praise The Lord! I am so ready for that surgery. I have a doctor appointment next Wednesday to discuss size of implants. I just pray they come out looking really nice.

July 19th

I had my pre-op appointment yesterday. My doctor said he would order an implant of around 700ccs for me. My surgery is a week from tomorrow. I am so looking forward to it. I'm ready to get these hard implants out. I will have my follow up appointment with another doctor, as my regular doctor will be on vacation. I know her as well from the coffee shop.

July 23rd

Yesterday I was so worn out and sore, I wasn't planning to go to church. The morning shift girl had been off all week and I had worked a lot. And that was all after I had my last fill-up of 100ccs! But Mike called and said that worship was awesome, so I threw on some clothes and ran a comb through my hair and went.

It was good. As I was sitting there at prayer time, I had thought about going up for prayer. But our pastor had called specific people up and I just didn't feel right about it. I guess I was kind of hoping that he would call me up too. But he didn't. He probably doesn't know I'm having surgery.

Anyway I was just sitting there, feeling worn out, when a dear friend (who has given me encouraging words before) comes and sits by me. She said the Lord just tapped on her shoulder and said, "Go and pray with Martha for renewed strength." And, so she did. I started to cry. I told her it was **exactly** what I needed. Even now, as I write about it in here, I feel so blessed. How awesome and amazing God is to think of me and to tell her to pray for me. What a blessing that she heard His voice and obeyed! Lord, I pray that I would hear your voice and obey when you tell me to bless someone else, through prayer or whatever it may be. Thank you Lord for your love, your everlasting and faithful love for me. I LOVE YOU!

July 25th

The afternoon shift girl at work had to quit work as she has been dizzy and not doing well. So, that means I am working alone at work all week, as the morning shift girl can't work past 1 pm. So I am back to my old shift of 1-5:30 pm, working and closing by myself.

I have been whining and complaining....a lot....blaming others for not being there to help me. I'm sorry Lord. That's wrong. I can't look to others to be my help and rescuer. **The Lord is my strength and my salvation**—not man.

---

2 Chronicles 16:9: "For the eyes of The Lord range through out the earth to strengthen those whose hearts are fully committed to Him".

July 26th

Tomorrow is my surgery. I pray that all goes well and good! Work has been absolutely crazy busy. I am so sore and wore out! One more day to go.

I asked for two weeks off, but my supervisors gave me three weeks. They said they don't want me to come back until I am ready to come back at full speed. It kind of hurt my feelings. It's like they're saying, don't even bother coming back at all unless you're ready to work your regular or more hours. What's wrong with me starting out at less and working up? I think I've proved myself this last month. I've worked **many** days all by myself, even though I am still sore. I feel like they're tired of me and my physical condition and don't want to deal with it anymore.

I am wondering and praying if it is time to move on? There are two job openings as a PAR—one in oncology and one in Team A. I almost feel like the coffee shop doesn't fit me anymore.

Please Lord; show me what I should do. I need your wisdom and counsel. Please guide the doctor's hands tomorrow during surgery. I pray I come out very happy and satisfied with my new breasts and Mike too. And, please give me strength for today to get through work. I pray it's not as busy as yesterday. Let it be a good day please. I love you, my Lord, my Savior, my friend, my confidant, my protector, my redeemer, my everything.

July 28th

Well, I had surgery yesterday. It went really well. I checked in for surgery at 12:30 p.m. and was going home by 5:30 p.m. Mike was a little worried about recovery, since I had such a hard time at my last one. But I came right out of it. Thank you Lord!

I think surgery was a little over an hour long. My surgeon had numbed me up pretty good, so I didn't really start hurting until around 6 a.m. this morning. I have been very sore today. I haven't been able to look at myself yet. Tomorrow I can take off my pink tube top and put on a sports bra. My surgeon had to open up the pocket a little more on my right side to match it with the left. The left side was a little lower.

So, tomorrow is the big day. The revealing! One thing I noticed right away was how nice to be rid of the hard unmoving rocks on my chest! I could move my back again. I didn't fall asleep until after 3 a.m. this morning. I wasn't really hurting, just couldn't sleep.

July 31st

Well, it's Tuesday. I had surgery on Friday. Jami called to see how I was doing, other than that, no one has called. I know I am feeling sorry for myself, but it's like no one cares how I am doing. I'm sorry Lord for my pity party. I was really down yesterday. There's a lot of emotion I am feeling with this surgery. I feel like people think it's not important anymore, that I'm not important anymore. I feel worthless. I'm tired of feeling down physically and emotionally.

Mike and I took off my tube top on Sunday. They are a bit bruised and you can see where the surgeon made the pocket bigger under my right side. They seem to match up pretty good. They seem so small though, compared to how big and hard they were before. So, there's mixed emotions about that. Will they be big enough? Will they "settle down" to look natural?

Jami called just now, and we had a good talk. It made me feel better. It's a beautiful day outside. Thank you Lord for lifting my spirits through talking to Jami.

AUGUST 2007

Aug. 8ᵗʰ

Ephesians 6:10: God's word teaches, "Be strong in The Lord (be empowered through your union with Him); draw your strength from Him (that strength which His boundless might provides)". We are to put on God's armor so we won't be deceived by the devil. Verse 16 says, "Lift up over all the (covering) shield of saving faith, upon which you can quench all the flaming missiles of the wicked (one)."

Psalm 27:1, 4: "The Lord is my light and my salvation— whom shall I fear? The Lord is the stronghold of my life— of whom shall I be afraid? One thing I ask of The Lord, this is what I seek: that I may dwell in the house of The Lord all the days of my life, to gaze upon the beauty of The Lord and to seek Him in His temple.......at His tabernacle I will sacrifice with shouts of joy; I will sing and make music to The Lord."

Psalm 28:6-7: "Praise be to The Lord, for He has heard my cry for mercy. The Lord is my strength and my shield. My heart trusts in Him and I am helped!! My heart leaps for joy and I will give thanks to Him in song."

Psalm 30:4: "Sing to The Lord, you saints of His; praise His holy name. For His anger lasts only a moment, but His favor lasts a lifetime; weeping may remain for a night, but rejoicing comes in the morning." (vs. 11) "You turned my wailing into dancing; you removed my sackcloth and clothed me with joy, that my heart may sing to you and not be silent. O Lord my God, I will give you thanks forever."

Aug. 21st

Let's see—no baby yet. Jami is now past her due date and miserable. We drove over to Pullman last weekend to help Jacob move over there. He started school yesterday. He has a new girlfriend now, Alicia. We have known her parents since they first got married. God is awesome and yet He also surprises us. Jacob thought he would move away and find a girl from somewhere (anywhere else, he said) other than Kelso, Longview area. Well, guess what? That didn't happen. She's very beautiful and friendly, but a little on the quiet side. She goes to WSU in Vancouver.

Josiah got a job in Seattle a couple of weeks ago and moved out. But, he comes home today to get all of his things. I pick him up from the train station here in a couple of hours. Isaiah is still here, until next month, where he will be moving to Portland to go The Art Institute. It will be so strange to have everyone gone and sad too.

I am healing well. I go back to work a week from today. At my post-op appointment, the surgeon I saw gave me four weeks off. The other girl working at the coffee shop will be gone and I will start back on eight-hour days. I think I will be sore, but okay.

The Lord blessed me with a $300 bonus check through work, which paid for my airfare to Jami's. Thank you Lord! Then, I also received a check from my short term disability insurance company. Another blessing.

SEPTEMBER 2007

Sept. 5th

Let's see, I went back to work last week. I worked eight-hour days with the two new girls. They are both young, but they are good workers and smart. I was VERY TIRED, but I made it.

Jami finally had the baby a week ago today. Ahriel Anita—9lbs, 6oz, 20 inches long, and very bruised. She's looking much better now. Aliyah is so proud of her and loves her so much. Abby likes to slap her and rough house with her. Abby is only 16 months old. She'll get better with her. Abby had surgery yesterday—drain tubes in both ears and her adenoids removed. Jami sent pictures. She was pretty swollen up. Jami said she acted like a little drunk girl because of the anesthesia.

Psalm 55:22: "Cast your cares on The Lord and He will sustain you. He will never let the righteous fall.....But as for me, I trust in you."

2 Cor. 12:10: "For when I am weak, then I am strong".

"Lord, grant me the serenity to accept the things I cannot change, the courage to change the things I can, and the wisdom to know the difference". (Serenity Prayer)

OCTOBER 2007

Oct. 25th

Went to see my surgeon yesterday about my next surgery, reconstruction of nipples. My left side is tighter and does not drop down as low as my right. My doctor says it is because of scar tissue from my breast reduction. So, he said we will wait until January to see how things look then. He said he can do some type of "Z" incision to help relax the skin and hopefully that will work. We'll just have to wait and see.

Oct. 26th

(An old song) "Yesterday's gone, sweet Jesus. And tomorrow may never be mine. So, help me today, give me the strength, one day at a time".

I just felt The Lord was reminding me how all I really have is today, right now, this moment. So, make the best of it. I seem to live in the future A LOT. I think things like, "When I lose weight, I'll do this and this and things will be better," etc. I think the more we live for the future, we spend less time and energy and focus on today and today's issues and struggles.

How can we "Put up the good fight" with all our strength and effort, if we're constantly thinking about tomorrow, next week, next month, next summer, etc? God's mercies are new every day, but they're only for today. So, help me

Lord to remember, I need your mercy and grace and strength for today's struggles and battles. As Jesus said— "Don't worry about tomorrow, today has enough worries of it's own to deal with". Jesus, you are so wise.

Oct. 29th

I felt The Lord showed me how I have never in my life been content with my body. I've always felt I was too tall, too big boned, too fat, too flabby, too white skinned, etc. I have always tried to be content with the things I had. I've always known a bigger house, fancier car, more money, etc, would never make me happy. If I received them, I would be thankful, but not a happier, more content person. Not so with my physical body. I have never been content with my physical body. I've always thought I'd be happier and more content, if I weighed less or looked different.

I asked God for His forgiveness for never being content or satisfied with how I am built or where my body is at the moment. (Content—to be satisfied with what one has) (Satisfy—to put an end to a demand or craving by giving what is required—to demand no more than this, to consider that this is enough) I remember hearing across the pulpit in a sermon that contentment is wanting what you have.

I've always said I will never give up the fight of losing weight and being thinner. When The Lord said to give my weight to Him, it was not a "giving up," but a "giving over." He will fight the fight for me. All I need to do is keep my eyes on Him and seek first The Kingdom of God. Then all things will be added.

The Lord just wants me to be happy, healthy, content, and satisfied right now—today—with where I am at physically. Stop striving, be still, and know that He is God. (Psalm 46:10)

I am feeling a lot less stress and not wanting to binge eat or shove food in my face. I want to taste and enjoy what I am eating. Live for today—be satisfied and content. Thank you Lord for what you are revealing to me. I know you want only the best for me.

DECEMBER 2007

Dec. 19th

Zephaniah 3:17: "Do not fear, O Zion. The Lord your God is with you, He is mighty to save. He will take great delight in you, He will quiet you with His love, He will rejoice over you with singing."

Journal Entry
JANUARY 2008

Jan. 2nd

A new year, a new beginning. Praise the Lord for His mercies, new every day. The last time I wrote in here, I felt God told me to give him my weight, to stop striving and just live. I still believe that, but I really need some help getting back on track with healthy eating.

So I joined Healthy Way. I have my first meeting today and will start the program tomorrow. I have gained a lot of weight this last year. It seems all the other times I've joined a diet group, I've always thought, *Man, I'm going to get skinny!* I am not feeling that way this time. I want to get healthy. I want to eat healthy, get in shape, and be more physically active. I am not concerned about the end goal weight. But, I definitely need help doing it. I am looking forward to feeling better. I ache a lot right now and mentally I feel tired and run down. I know it's because of the way I've been eating.

I also start school on Monday. A math class and two health classes, working towards a Medical Assisting AA Degree. We fly out to see Jami, Jose and girls on Jami's birthday in February! I feel this year is the year of new beginnings for me. Then Mike told me the number eight means new beginnings—resurrection. How cool is that?

I still have my last surgery, probably in March on Easter weekend. Another cool thing! My mastectomy surgery was on Easter weekend last year and to finish up on Easter weekend again. I know it's God. GOD IS SO AWESOME!

FEBRUARY 2008

Feb.4th

<u>Psalms 28:6, 7</u>: "Praise be to The Lord for He has heard my cry for mercy. The Lord is my strength and my shield, my heart trusts in Him and I am helped. My heart leaps for joy and I will give thanks to Him in song".

MARCH 2008

March 17th

Blessed be The Lord! Today and forever!

Just thought I'd bring my journal up to date. My last surgery is this Friday—Good Friday—Easter weekend. Just like it began on Easter weekend, so it finishes on Easter, too. God is so awesome! What a reminder of His love, goodness, mercy and new beginnings and new life! I will be getting my "headlights," as Mike calls them.

Yesterday in church I wanted prayer, but there wasn't a ministry time. But, the pastor had a musician play his clarinet while he read scripture over all of us as a body. I just felt and saw God putting a blanket over me, a covering of protection and warmth and peace. So, I was ministered to. God is so good.

I took my math final last week, so I am done with school, for this quarter. Woo hoo!

I have been going to Healthy Way for ten weeks now and have lost around twenty-three pounds. I feel so much better. I went shopping this weekend and bought a couple of shirts. We had a wonderful visit with Jami, Jose and the girls. I really miss them. I just hope and pray they'll come out this summer. We are also (Mike and I) going to try to go to Hawaii this summer for our 30th anniversary. Well, that's about it for now. I love you Lord!

March 27th

Well, I had my last surgery a week ago, last Friday, March 21st. I had to be there at 6 am, surgery was at 7:30am. I woke up in recovery at 10:30 am and was home by 12:30pm. So, it went fast. My skin grafts are really high up in my groin area. The surgeon used the skin from here as it is a naturally darker color and resembles the texture and color of the nipple and areola.

I am pretty sore and walk like I rode a horse too long. I had my post-op appointment yesterday. My surgeon took off the bandages around my new nipples. He removed some stitches but not all of them. He did several incisions in the lower left side to try and relax the scar tissue there. I have to go in on Monday to have them removed.

The surgeon and his MA both thought everything looked really good. I thought my new nipples looked a little freakish. They are really long, but they said they shrink A LOT so that's why he made them so long. He gave me 2 pieces of foam with little holes cut out of the middle to place over the nipple to protect it from getting squished down.

March 27th

Last night, I put the little sponges on and then a sports bra and went to bed. I had a dream that both sides fell off and I was trying to find my doctor to sew them back on. I woke up and my bra felt too tight, so I took it off. Strange dream, I know it was because I was worried about them.

Mike says they remind him of when I had my breast reduction as they were bruised and looked beat up. They had removed my nipples and then did the reduction, then sewed them back on. Anyway, they look weird, but the surgeon and medical assistant said they looked good. I don't have anything to compare them too, having never seen any pictures. I just hope and pray everything comes out looking good. *(This was the last entry in my journal)*

I had the option of getting the area tattooed, but at the time I felt the skin color was dark enough for me already. But, five years has passed now and they have lightened up quite a bit. So now I am reconsidering getting them tattooed. As I had said, the nipples were really long, but they did shrink a lot. It was a good thing they were long to begin with. The area is numb just like the rest of my breasts. The scars have faded tremendously though. The left side is still slightly higher than the right and causes me more discomfort from the scar tissue that is there; all small prices to pay I feel for having my life. I will never have to wear a bra again though, and that causes me no grief.

AFTERWORD

As I read back through this booklet, I see Jesus all over it. This is my journal of what happened to me, but it's really not about me at all. It's all about God and how He was always there, how He paved the way, how He walked with me, how faithful and loving He is. It amazes me every time I read this how much He loves me and wants to be there for me and help me through the difficult times. Now here is the best part of all, Jesus is there for EVERYONE! He loves all of you, too! He wants to show you His love by being there for you through your difficult times. He wants to show His faithfulness, grace, and mercy to YOU, the reader.

So if you don't know Jesus as your personal savior, friend, confidant, redeemer, and oh so much more, then I want to extend an invitation to you. All we have to do is ask. His salvation, love, grace, mercy are all FREE! He already paid the price by giving His life at the cross. It cost Him everything, but it's free to us. There is nothing we can do to earn it, nothing. He just wants us to come to Him and open our hearts up and invite Him in. So simple really, yet so hard for most of us.

I know it was hard for me, as I kept waiting, feeling too unworthy, too messed up, too imperfect to come to Him. How could He love me? Didn't He know all the bad things I had done? Didn't He know all the horrible thoughts that went through my mind? Oh, He knows. We can't hide anything from Him. But He loves us anyways. That's the miracle! It was a big risk to take, to open up my heart and invite Jesus in. It was the biggest risk I had taken at that point in my life at the age of nineteen. It was the best decision I have ever made.

My prayer for you is that you will take that risk too and ask Jesus into your hearts. Your life will never be the same, and you will begin on an incredible journey. It's definitely worth the risk.

Psalm 73:23-26: "Yet I am always with you, you hold me by my right hand. You guide me with your counsel, and afterward you will take me into glory. Whom have I but you? And earth has nothing I desire besides you. My flesh and my heart may fail, but God is the strength of my heart and my portion forever."

ABOUT THE AUTHOR

Martha Sherman is married and lives with her husband in the beautiful Pacific Northwest. Together they have four children, three of which are married, and five grandchildren. She earned her Medical Assistant Certificate in 2010 and continues to work at the same hospital where she has been employed for almost ten years. She thoroughly enjoys her job as she gets to serve others, which is one of her greatest joys.

To contact Martha please feel free to email her at: marthaksherman@gmail.com